First Published in the UK in 2015 by Focus Education (UK) Ltd
Revised November 2016

Focus Education (UK) Ltd
Publishing
Talking Point Conference & Exhibition Centre
Huddersfield Road
Scouthead
Saddleworth
OL4 4AG

Focus Education (UK) Ltd Reg. No 4507968

ISBN 978-1-909038-65-3

Companies, institutions and other organisations wishing to make bulk purchases of books published by Focus Education should contact their local bookstore or Focus Education direct:

Customer Services, Focus Education, Talking Point Conference & Exhibition Centre, Huddersfield Road, Scouthead, Saddleworth, OL4 4AG
Tel 01457 821818 Fax 01457 878205

www.focus-education.co.uk
customerservice@focus-education.co.uk
Printed in Great Britain by Blueprint Creative Media, Stockport

focuseducationuk

focuseducation1

focus-education-uk-ltd

CW01112640

ABOUT THE AUTHOR

CLIVE DAVIES OBE

Clive Davies has a vast experience in primary education. He has inspected more than 200 schools. Whilst a headteacher Clive's school gained a National Curriculum award and his school was featured in the Times Educational Supplement as one of 3 recognised for its quality practice. The development of pupil autonomy was at the heart of the culture of his successful headships. Clive is well known nationally and internationally having worked in schools throughout England and Wales as well as Dubai, Kuwait, Greece, Turkey, Holland, Cyprus, Germany and Spain. He was awarded an OBE for his services to education in 2007.

Contents

Many thanks.........

- In compiling this publication I have received much support from the schools outlined to the right.

- Many thanks to all the staff from these schools for the valuable contributions, including discussions, which have helped to shape my thinking.

- In addition, I would like to thank every member of the Focus team: consultants; associate consultants and of course the office team.

The following schools have contributed to this publication:

- Roundthorn Primary Academy, Oldham

- Glodwick Infant School, Oldham

- Colley Lane Primary, West Midlands

- St Joseph's Catholic Primary, Leigh

- English Martyrs' RC Primary, Derbyshire

- St Teresa's RC Primary, Nottingham

- Selwyn Primary, Newham

4

Making Book Scrutiny More Meaningful

Linking Book Scrutiny to Teaching Judgements

Introduction

Why the growing importance of Book Scrutiny?

- Recent changes to the inspection framework has made it clear that: when judging teaching over time more weight needs to be given to the evidence of learning as evidenced in learners' books.

- This should naturally lead to much more focus being given to book scrutiny as a natural part of a school's self evaluation process.

- In addition, monitoring arrangements need to be adjusted to give greater emphasis to book scrutiny.

- This publication is aimed at helping school leaders be more effective and efficient in their book scrutiny activities.

Ofsted

Key Ofsted inspection messages

- Spend more time **looking at a range of pupils' work** in order to consider what progress they are making in different areas of the curriculum.

- Be clear about how you **use of formative and summative assessment to improve teaching and to raise achievement.**

- Evaluate how pupils are doing against **age related expectations**, as set in the National Curriculum.

- Consider how you use assessment information **to identify pupils who are falling behind** in their learning and need additional support to reach their full potential, including more able.

What should we be focusing on during a Book Scrutiny?

Using Book Scrutiny as a monitoring tool:

What you need to know:

- Your main focus needs to be:

- How well are pupils making progress?

- Are all pupils making enough progress?

- Is the teaching effective enough to enable learners to maximise their progress?

- What standards pupils ought to be attaining

- Year group expectations for reading, writing and mathematics

- What were their latest end of year standards

- If there significant variations across different groups of learners

- Whether there is evidence of deep learning

How can we ensure that we use our time effectively?

Decide your focus and stick to it !

- Even those with the clearest intentions can be distracted from the core purpose of the scrutiny and end up focusing their attention on presentation, handwriting, spelling and marking.

- These are all important factors and you will have agreed school guidelines and expectations relating to them.

- They all need monitoring in their own right but it is important that they do not become the focus of every book scrutiny.

What should we be considering?

When carrying out any book scrutiny consider the following:

Focus	• Decide your focus. • Keep the focus tight and don't try to look at too many things at once.
Sample	• Decide which sample of pupils' work you are looking at. Consider carefully which work will give you the best evidence base to deal with your chosen issue. • Consider which groups of pupils need to be represented in the scrutiny, e.g. random, gender specific, under-performing, SEN, least able, more able, most able, EAL learners, ethnic groups etc.
Time limit	• Decide how long you are allocating to complete the scrutiny and stick to it. On the whole a work scrutiny for a single issue shouldn't take much longer than one hour. If it does, your focus may be too broad.

Which documentation may be useful?

It can be helpful to have some basic documentation to hand which can support a book scrutiny:

RAISEonline/ Inspection Dashboard	Consider conversion rates, group achievement – boys/ girls; disadvantaged/ no disadvantage; lower attainers/ high attainers; etc.
Year Group Expectations	Knowledge of Year Group Expectations will be a *must* when making judgements about standards and achievement. Part Two of this publications sets these out for you and should help you to recognise how well pupils are doing in relation to them.
Planning	Planning documentation can be helpful for some book scrutinies, e.g. if you are looking at differentiation, it may be helpful to compare the planning with the written outcomes.
Assessment Data	Sometimes it is helpful to know the most recent assessment outcomes for the pupils you are looking at to provide a context for their work.
Compare outcomes from scrutiny with targets	Compare the outcomes as indicated in the work books against the targets that may set for individuals, groups or full classes. Look at both numerical targets and curricular targets.

How can we gain greater impact with Book Scrutiny?

One of the ways in which schools and academies have had greatest impact with book scrutiny is to set up a situation where teachers are used to having their books looked at.

There are several ways of achieving this in a non-threatening way. An example of this is outlined below:

- Fortnightly impact meetings with a colleague focusing on book scrutiny. One colleague brings a pre-agreed set of books to the first meeting and then they alternate at their next meeting. Pairs should not be 'experienced' and 'less experienced' teachers but teachers should have a certain amount of freedom to choose their own partners.

- This should then be followed up with 'half termly' pupil progress meetings with phase leaders.

- Leading to termly summative pupil progress meeting with the headteacher/ principal.

In this way teachers get used to their books being a major focus when looking at the impact their teaching is having.

Making Book Scrutiny More Meaningful

Linking Book Scrutiny to Teaching Judgements

Part One:

What are we looking for?

The Strands to Focus on:

1. Marking and Feedback
2. Presentation
3. Lesson Design
4. High Expectation and Challenge
5. Differentiation
6. Progress
7. Appropriate Praise

The Strands to Focus on:

1	Marking and Feedback	1.1	Is marking up to date and in line with the school's policy?
		1.2	Are responses to pupils' learning helping them make progress by identifying at least one key area for improvement?
		1.3	Are 'barriers to learning' being identified and then used to plan future learning?
2	Presentation	2.1	Is the learning appropriately dated and does presentation meets the school's expectations?
		2.2	Is there evidence that basic handwriting, spelling and grammar are improving?
3	Lesson Design	3.1	Are learning objectives very clearly linked to the learning outcomes?
		3.2	Is there evidence of practise and consolidation, where it is appropriate?
		3.3	Is there evidence of the principles of British Values being adhered to?
4	High Expectations and Challenge	4.1	Is the worked completed/ planned linked directly to year group expectations?
		4.2	Is there evidence of high expectations and learning being challenging enough?
		4.3	Is there, through the feedback, marking and type of learning provided, evidence of a culture and ethos of scholastic excellence being promoted?

The Strands to Focus on:

5	Differentiation	5.1	Is there evidence that those requiring intervention are being identified so that all learners keep up?
		5.2	Is learning appropriately differentiated with evidence conclusive within different books?
		5.3	Is there evidence that differentiation is achieved by emphasising deep knowledge and through individual support and intervention?
		5.4	Is there evidence of deep learning, especially for more able learners?
6	Progress	6.1	Is there evidence that pupils' understanding during a lesson is being systematically checked and adjustments made as needed?
		6.2	Are there procedures in place to help learners know exactly what they need to achieve?
		6.3	Is there conclusive evidence of pupils demonstrating sufficient gains in knowledge, skills and understanding?
		6.4	Has progress been rapid enough from the beginning of the year; and last half term to the present day?
7	Appropriate Praise	7.1	Is there evidence of a climate being created where pupils' learning, in the form of finished outcomes, is really valued?
		7.2	Is there evidence that learners' successes are being 'celebrated'?

Strand 1

Marking and Feedback

1.1   Is marking up to date and in line with the school's policy?

1.2   Are responses to pupils' learning helping them make progress by identifying at least one key area for improvement?

1.3   Are 'barriers to learning' being identified and then used to plan future learning?

Strand 1   Marking and Feedback

1.1   Is marking and feedback up to date and in line with an effective school policy?

Inadequate	Requires Improvement	Good	Outstanding
• Feedback does not consistently comply with school policy.	• Feedback is mainly compliant with school policy.	• Feedback is compliant with school policy.	• Feedback provides exemplary evidence against school policy.
• There are a number of consecutive pages that have no remarks from the teacher.	• Although work is marked regularly the remarks are mostly just responding with remarks of how well they have done, ie, 'I am pleased with the effort you put in', etc.	• Books have been marked regularly.	• There is evidence of consistent adherence to a system that is supporting pupils' learning by indicating how they could improve their standard of work.
• Too many pages have short responses such as 'well done' or 'see me'.		• The marking is consistent across the class.	
• There are occasional examples of incorrect work being marked correctly.	• There is little evidence that the marking links to improvement made or aids future improvement.	• There is good attention to linking the comments to the initial learning objectives the pupils had.	• There are guided opportunities for pupils to improve on an aspect of their learning.
• Marking is not up-to-date.		• There is clear indication as to what needs addressing in the future.	
• Not all learners know how well they have done and what they need to do improve their work.	• Marking tends to be inconsistent across different subjects.	• Work is marked against the learning objective and success criteria, and focused on learning outcomes.	• There is substantial evidence that pupils have been given the opportunity to address potential improvements at a later stage.
• Learners' progress is being inhibited because of the inconsistencies in marking and feedback	• Agreed aspects such as self-assessment and peer assessment have not been sustained for lengthy periods.	• Feedback to individuals is easy to follow and helpful in relation to improving future work.	• Written feedback provides excellent information regarding the level the learners are working at.
	• Although evidence of effective marking exist, there is a lack of consistency in its application.	• Scrutiny of workbooks reveals that work has been accurately assessed.	• Written feedback is linked to clear, user-friendly statements, that learners understand.
		• Assessment information is being used well to inform planning and to focus on future improvement.	

Strand 1   Marking and Feedback

1.2   Are responses to pupils' learning helping them make progress by identifying at least one key area for improvement?

Inadequate	Requires Improvement	Good	Outstanding
• There is little or no evidence that marking or feedback is making a difference to the progress being made. • Work is not always appropriately and accurately marked with little evidence of the next stage of learning and/or misconception being identified. • There are several examples of the same mistake being made with little evidence of sustained improvement or response to any remarks made by the teacher. • There is little evidence that learners are being provided with opportunities to reflect on previous learning and learn from it. • Marking lacks focus and does not help the learner.	• The feedback provided does not make it clear how improvement can be achieved. • Written feedback does not always provide helpful comments on how well learners have done and how they can improve their work and make progress towards personal targets. • Despite examples of feedback (in written format) given, there is inconsistent evidence of improvement overall. • Any improvement as a result of feedback is not always sustained for any length of time. • Impact on progress is therefore too often 'short term'. • There is limited evidence of self assessment or peer marking	• Work is appropriately and accurately marked with evidence of the next stage of learning and/or misconception being identified. • Feedback addresses basic skill errors as well as the focus of the objective. • In most cases, there is considered and immediate response from pupils to the feedback received and future work shows that much of this has been sustained. • Due to the fact that the feedback directly relates to the year's objectives it is clear that progress is being made toward the National Standard. • Assessment information is being used well to inform future planning and next stage of learning.	• There is evidence of excellent opportunities being provided for learners to evaluate how they have improved as a result of the feedback provided. • As a result of this feedback there is very positive impact being made on the progress. • The intended improvement can be directly linked to the year objectives. • Where appropriate, peer marking is used most effectively. • Written feedback is linked to clear, user-friendly statements that learners understand. • There is an expectation that younger learners share ideas with talk/writing partners and consequently they share opinion on each others' learning.

Queen Diana was very greedy and selfish and didn't want anyone to inherit her beauty. So we banished her son Prince Salum to a rugg with [all was soon]

quite

Excellent! You have described your second well using fantastic adjectives.

Next steps:

* Up-level this sentence Junaid. Try and use better adjectives.

* His finger pointed like a pencil that were sharp from each finger.

Thursday 8th October

Example of a learner being asked to improve one part of their writing. In this case, it is linked to improving their description.

Year 6 (September) – recounting experience of tackling a 'climbing wall'
An example of the teacher directing a pupil to focus on an area that requires
improvement and of the pupil responding to the teacher's request.

There is evidence of an opportunities being provided for learners to evaluate how
they have improved as a result of the feedback provided.

After I got down I was prod of w
I achevied.

Rewrite this final paragraph to add more
description of your sense of achievement.

Once I got down I felt extrordirary f
What I had just achevied! Now that I had be
up once, I wanted to go up again and agai

Strand 1   Marking and Feedback

1.3   Are 'barriers to learning' being identified and then used to plan future learning?

Inadequate	Requires Improvement	Good	Outstanding
• There is little evidence of the marking identifying any areas for improvement let alone being diagnostic enough to identify barriers to learning. • Marking does not link to the focus of the learning. • Marking does not help learners know if they have been successful in meeting the objectives set. • There is no evidence that as a result of the previous learning adjustments have been made to any new learning planned or delivered. • There is little evidence that the teacher is making use of the information held about learners' level of attainment when making remarks about work or when planning future learning.	• Although work is marked on a regular basis there is not enough evidence that it is impacting on future learning. • Teachers are not consistent in using data to help assess learners' relative progress. • The lack of challenge in on-going work is as a result of a failure to identify precisely the next area of learning for individuals. • Targets are too generic and do not help to move on the learning. • There is a lack of awareness of the main trends in the most recent summative assessments and as a result the sequence of intended learning in a set of books does not follow a logic pattern.	• There is evidence that the outcomes of marking are being used to make decisions about future learning. • There is good awareness of each learners' level of attainment and this helps to provide clarity about the next area of learning. • There are good links made about the attainment in reading, writing and mathematics and therefore work across the curriculum is planned with this in mind. • Targets are appropriately linked to the identified barriers to learning for both writing and mathematics. • Teacher subject knowledge is good enough to allow for appropriate diagnosis of a subject.	• It is clear by looking at sequences of work in learners' books that you have made adjustments to your programme of learning to take full account of weaknesses and misconceptions that you have identified in previous work. • The misconceptions or mistakes made are linked directly to the outcomes from year group expectations which helps learners be focused on meeting the national standards. • It is evident that your subject knowledge is excellent and that you are able to provide the right level of support in future work, based on the errors identified in previous learning. • Marking is sharply diagnostic and constructive.

Non-Chronological Report

You MUST remember to use:

	Me	Partner	Teacher
		M. I Hilary	
The third person (no - I, you, me, we, us)	✓	✓	✓
Technical vocabulary - see your plan	✓	✓	✓
The present tense (is, are, has, have)	✓	✓	✓
One or two generalisers (the vast majority, mainly, most, usually, generally)	✓	✓	✓
Connectives to add information eg. additionally, furthermore	✓	✓	✓
Formal connectives ~ therefore, however, due to, despite, although	✓	✓	✓
Sentence types: one 'de:de' sentence, and one noun, which/where sentence.	✓	✓	de : de
Paragraphs	✓	✓	✓

To add / delete rows, click on the table – go to 'Table' – 'Insert / Delete'

→ Improve this paragraph. ① Is furthermore the best word to use here? Think about your connectives ② Check your paragraph for commas, especially where you have used a connective. ③ Be careful that you don't swap and change your ideas – I will explain this to the class.

Write it out again here –

Tuesday 14th October 14

/An extremely engaging report - I was fascinated! Well done Keira

Can I write an engaging report?

The Whispering Nightmare

The Whispering Nightmare (Volcanous Nightmarus) is a reptile and comes from the family Veronia. It was ordered onto (carnivorous and is a very rare sp creature, its species is Nightmare.

It lives on the remote island of Hunassii and exists in a cave buried beneath the side of a volcano 120 years ago Nightmares nested on the british isles such as this but...

As The Most of the Nightmares live in a hot climate so they can incubate their eggs with...

The Whispering Nightmare has generally has molten skin which and Lava pulsing inside therefore this enables it scamper bright places. Its Icy scales are armour plated which makes it impenetrable... Nightmares (which ... flying over like rivers working to stab its victim. Nightmares normally 10m long and has a wing span of 3m and has a ceiling long tail. ✓

This amazing predator breathes fire and poison. Furthermore, Humans should not go near it. In contrast Inuit with sight cut to any nearby creature or mammal and hurt it. Volcanous Nightmarus has very good eyesight and has excellent speed and additionally very aggressive. The Whispering nightmare is very deadly, they squirt acid on any creature burning it from the inside. It has a life span of 900 years.

This dragon has no relation ship with humans eventhough Humans

Peer assessment used effectively to engage learners.

Dialogue between learner and teacher resulting in deeper thinking and consolidation of understanding

1 1 3 7 ✓

Pa: you have used the column method.
Jack Marshall

Year 3 ~ January

Gap Task
How could you check this answer is correct?
Do it the other way!

- Can you remember the correct word for that?
- What operation would you use?

yes its inverse.

X or ÷

Have a go at
this now you
have stuck it
in. You can do
it. :)

Thanks for beliving
in me that I can
do it! :)

Strand 2

Presentation

2.1   Is the learning appropriately dated and does presentation meet the school's expectations?

2.2   Is there evidence that basic handwriting, spelling and grammar are improving?

Strand 2   Presentation

2.1   Is the learning appropriately dated and does presentation meets the
school's expectations?

Inadequate	Requires Improvement	Good	Outstanding
• There is little evidence that learners are being encouraged to adhere to a system of presentation that matches that expected for their age. • There are few, if any, examples of poor handwriting or shoddy work being picked up, which leads to pupils often having work unfinished in their books and a standard of handwriting that is not appropriate.	• Although it is clear that there is an agreed system of presentation, adherence to this system is inconsistent. • There are occasional remarks made when the standard of presentation falls below that expected, however this is not a feature of the marking. • As a result of the lack of consistency, learners are not consistent in their presentation skills and sometimes fall below the standard expected for their age.	• All work is set out neatly and there is good evidence that learners take a pride in their final outcomes. • It is evident that learners know what is expected of them in relation to setting out their learning. • Systems that have been agreed are being adhered to, e.g. dating, underlining, etc. • When presentation falls below the expected standard there is evidence that this is being picked up and often remarked on in the books.	• Work is set out in an excellent manner giving the impression that learners take much pride in their work. • It is very evident that very high standards have been set for the way learners present their work and this is being adhered to by all learners in the class. • An appropriate and effective system of presentation is consistently adhered to, with no evidence of incomplete or shoddy work. • Learners conform with a system that clearly outlines the date the tasks were completed; learning objective/ challenges clearly indicated and new work clearly demarcated.

Strand 2   Presentation

2.2   Is there evidence that basic handwriting, spelling and grammar are improving?

Inadequate	Requires Improvement	Good	Outstanding
• Presentation is inconsistent and disappointing overall. • Learners are not being picked up for untidy work and therefore there is little evidence of improvement. • Learners' handwriting does not follow the agreed system used by the school. • There does not seem to be a process in place to improve learners' spelling, leading to spelling often being below the standard expected for their age. • There are many instances of shoddy and incomplete work throughout the learners' books. • There are examples of coloured in diagrams and illustrations being completed poorly.	• There is little evidence of improvement in overall presentation over time. • There is an attempt made to improve handwriting but it is clear that this is not consistently applied. • There is not a coherent system for dealing with mis-spelt words which leads to inconsistencies in spelling overall. • There is evidence of intermittent use of pencil and pen which leads to overall presentation being disappointing. • Although untidy and shoddy work is being commented upon it seems to make little difference to the next piece of work.	• It is clear that speaking and listening activities have been used to underpin writing activities which, in turn, complement the development of reading. • A consistent system of helping learners to spell correctly is in place. • The vast majority of words related to the National Curriculum spelling lists are being spelt correctly according to the age of the learners. • The standard of handwriting at least matches that expected of learners' age. • There is a consistent system in place for when a learner moves from pencil to pen.	• When taking account of the standard of work produced at the beginning of term there is evidence that there has been improvement in the presentation of work (or consistency for work already of a high standard). • Handwriting is consistent and, at least, matches the expectation for the age group. • It is clear that words that were spelt incorrectly early in the academic year are now being spelt correctly. • Grammatical features have improved in line with age expectations. • A system of rewarding pupils for neat presentation, e.g. 'awarding of a pen', is in place, which leads to learners striving to do their best.

Strand 3

Lesson Design

3.1   Are learning objectives very clearly linked to the learning outcomes?

3.2   Is there evidence of practise and consolidation, where it is appropriate?

3.3   Is there evidence of the principles of British Values being adhered to?

Strand 3   Lesson Design

3.1   Are learning objectives very clearly linked to the learning outcomes?

Inadequate	Requires Improvement	Good	Outstanding
• There is not a consistent system in place of using learning objectives. • Where learning objectives exist they do not clarify what is to be taught and therefore do not relate to learning that follows. • There are few examples if any of success criteria being identified. • There is inconsistent evidence that the learning relates directly to the age group expectations.	• The effective use of learning objectives and success criteria results in learners' making progress but there is a lack of consistency. • On most occasions the learning objective can be traced back to the teaching objectives in medium term plans. This can be variable. • On occasions the learning objective is expressed in such a way that it separates the learning from the context. There are also times when this is not the case. • It is not always clear that the learning objective and/or success criteria links directly to the work that follows.	• The use of learning objectives and success criteria helps learners to assess their own work and leads to accelerated progress. • There is a very good link between prior learning and the new learning objective and it is clear that learners understand this. • The use of well-targeted learning objectives and success criteria ensures that learners are fully and actively engaged in their learning. • The learning objective is expressed in such a way that it separates the learning from the context.	• It is very clear that the learning objectives and success criteria are used very effectively to maximise progress. • There is excellent synergy between the learning objective and the task that follows. • The link between previous learning and new learning is very explicit and evidenced consistently. • Learners use success criteria to evaluate their own and other's work and this leads to progress over time being outstanding. • It is evident that learners are able to make links between their prior learning, the new learning objective and the success criteria to assess outcomes. • Learners are regularly evaluating their learning against the success criteria, are highly critical and know what they need to do next in order to improve in age appropriate subject language.

Strand 3   Lesson Design

3.2   Is there evidence of practise and consolidation, where it is appropriate?

Inadequate	Requires Improvement	Good	Outstanding
• There is a sense of a lack of organisation in learners' daily and long term learning, leading to a lack of consistency in their ability to understand and return to previously taught concepts. • A lack of regular practise leads to confusion in learners' understanding. • There is limited systematic process in place to establish what learners have not fully understood and the learning is driven by a mid-term plan that is not responsive enough.	• There are times when learners are being asked to complete too many examples of the same learning when it is clear that they have understood the concept. • Although practise and consolidation are features of daily learning, learners do not always have an efficient method to carry out several tasks, especially in mathematics. • More able learners are not progressing at the pace they should because there is either a lack of practise and consolidation or too much of it. • Although there is regular use of practise and consolidation, there is no clear link towards developing mastery skills.	• There is conclusive evidence of 'practise and consolidation' being used purposefully to help improve standards. • Pupils are being provided with an efficient method of completing tasks. • As a result of practise and consolidation learners feel very secure about the methods they use to complete tasks in writing and mathematics.	• Evidence from teachers' books show that they provide opportunities for learners to consolidate their understanding by providing sufficient practise. • The balance between practise and consolidation and providing opportunities for deep learning, especially for more able pupils, is most evident and providing a platform for developing scholastic excellence. • In mathematics, it is very evident that teachers move learners onto efficient methods as soon as it is practical to do so. • It is evident that teachers use practise and consolidation as a natural part of their evolvement towards mastery.

Strand 3   Lesson Design

3.3   Is there evidence of the principles of British Values being adhered to?

Inadequate	Requires Improvement	Good	Outstanding
• There are missed opportunities to promote aspects related to equality of opportunity; being fair; setting out a balanced argument and respecting others.	• Although there is evidence of learning being planned around equality of opportunity; living in a fair and free society and respecting others, there is little opportunity to develop this beyond guided activities that fail to enable learners to express personal views.	• There is evidence that learners are encouraged to express their views.	• Learners' views are expressed within the context of 'what is a fair society'.
• There are very few opportunities taken to encourage learners to follow their own lines of enquiry.		• There is evidence that learners are provided with frameworks to sustain their personal points of view.	• Written evidence suggests that learners are being helped to take a pride in the values that our country holds dear.
• There is little evidence that learners have a clear understanding about the way our country is governed and why laws are important.	• Although different festivals and religious celebrations are studied there is limited evidence of learners being provided with opportunities to consider the similarities across different faiths.	• There is evidence that learners are helped to understand the principles of equality of opportunity.	• Balanced arguments reflect the fact that learners can set out different view points before coming to a personal conclusion.
• There is little or no evidence of learners' personal views being valued.		• Younger learners are able to recognise that there are many people around them that help them.	• It is clear that learners are helped to respect the laws of the land and the people that are there to uphold these rules and the law.
	• There are occasions when it is clear that learners' personal views of being valued but there are also many missed opportunities for this to be promoted.	• There is evidence that learners have been involved in learning which helps them to keep safe.	• There are many opportunities provided for learners to follow their own lines of enquiry.
		• Learners have been helped to understand why we support various charities.	• There is huge respect for the principle of having a democracy, which includes a positive view of the monarchy.
		• There are opportunities provided for learners to follow their own research.	

Strand 4

High Expectations and Challenge

4.1   Is the worked completed/ planned linked directly to year group expectations?

4.2   Is there evidence of high expectations and learning being challenging enough?

4.3   Is there, through the feedback, marking and type of learning provided, evidence of a culture and ethos of scholastic excellence being promoted?

Strand 4   High Expectations and Challenge

4.1   Is the worked completed/ planned linked directly to year group expectations?

Inadequate	Requires Improvement	Good	Outstanding
• There is little evidence to suggest that you plan against the year group expectations and learners are therefore not being provided with appropriate opportunities to meet the expectations for their age group. • Standards are not being improved because there are gaps in pupils' learning due to a lack of a system that ensures that coverage is appropriate an teacher understanding of the next steps is insecure.	• Although teachers have awareness of year group expectations it is not always clear that they work directly to these expectations. • Not enough of the teachers' learning objectives can be traced back to link directly to year group expectations. • All the learning can be traced directly back to the National Curriculum's expectations, however the pace of the work will not guarantee that all expectations will be met before the end of the year. • There are examples of learning taking place which do not link directly to the National Curriculum's expectations.	• It is evident that teachers are familiar with the national expectations for the year/s group/s they teach and that almost all objectives can be traced back to link directly to year group expectations. • All the learning can be traced directly back to the National Curriculum's expectations for each age group and the pace is sufficient to ensure everything is being covered within each year. • There is a systematic approach to the programme of learning which ensures that there is enough time for practise and consolidation.	• It is evident that teachers are confident with the national expectations for the year/s group/s they teach and that all objectives can be traced back to link directly to year group expectations. • There is evidence that the teachers are 'teaching to the top' as outlined in the National Curriculum's recommendations. • It is evident that the tasks undertaken helps individuals to improve their knowledge, skills and understanding, linked directly to the National Curriculum and to their specific age group. • The pace of learning is clearly very demanding and ensures that learners will have met the year group objectives before the end of the year.

Strand 4   High Expectations and Challenge

4.2   Is there evidence of high expectations and learning being challenging enough?

Inadequate	Requires Improvement	Good	Outstanding
• There are several examples of learners not being challenged appropriately, leading to page after page of tasks being marked correct without accelerated progress being evident. • More able learners have not been provided with opportunities to deepen their learning and therefore tend to cover the same tasks for too long. • There is little evidence of enough flexibility being allowed and learners complete tasks that do not move on their knowledge, skills or understanding. • The challenge is too great owing to the lack of knowledge and skills needed to make progress.	• The range of activities undertaken does not guarantee that there are opportunities to deepen the learning for all pupils. • There are examples of the teachers sticking rigidly to a plan which has a detrimental impact on the progress made by learners. • There are examples of learners having completed too many of the same task, with all being marked correct, when they could have been moved on to more demanding tasks. • Planning is too rigid and does not allow for learners to be provided with time for consolidation or additional challenge, when needed.	• The setting of demanding objectives and awareness of the needs of different ability groups leads to progress being at least good on a short and long term basis. • Expectations are high with learners completing what is expected, both in terms of quantity and quality within each lesson. • The learning objective makes it clear what is expected of the learners. • The activities are suitably differentiated and meet the needs of the different learners. • There is evidence of the teacher being flexible when the occasion demands.	• Good use is made of information about the prior learning of individuals leads to activities being pitched at the right level leading to learners making excellent progress both in the short and long term. • It is evident that the teacher is aware of the learners' prior learning and attainment and has organised activities that take that into account. • It is evident that learners work at a brisk pace and that they have a clear understanding of what is expected of them. • The tasks have been organised well to take account of all abilities. • There is a real sense of the learners knowing exactly what they need to do to improve. • There is evidence that many of the tasks are open-ended and requires deep thinking on behalf of the learner.

Strand 4　High Expectations and Challenge

4.3　Is there, through the feedback, marking and type of learning provided, evidence of a culture and ethos of scholastic excellence being promoted?

Inadequate	Requires Improvement	Good	Outstanding
• It is evident that there is a lack of subject knowledge and therefore an inflexible approach to the tasks that the learners undertake. • Learners do not see themselves as historians, geographers or scientists but instead 'do' history, geography and science. • Learners are not being supported to have a love for learning and see tasks as something that has to be completed rather than about something that would enhance their knowledge, skills and understanding.	• Whilst activities can be demanding, there is little sense that learners are being supported to see themselves as being excellent in any subject. • Individual subjects are being covered appropriately but few learners would carry on learning beyond the classroom. • There is little to suggest that learners have embraced a culture of enjoying literature. • Little suggests that learners have been provided with opportunities to deepen their knowledge, skills and understanding in any subject.	• It is evident that teachers are able to move away from the original plan if need be to challenge more able learners more effectively. • Good understanding of how children learn ensures that teaching is adapted to suit any situation. • It is evident that learners' knowledge and understanding has been deepened across a range of subjects. • There is evidence of enough flexibility in planning to allow for accelerated progress in a given area. • Learners are aided to embrace the concept of being 'long-life' readers. • There is a good sense that learners enjoy 'challenging' tasks and are not over-faced by them.	• It is evident that the excitement about the subject being taught is infectious, leading to many learners pursuing an interest beyond the classroom. • Learners are helped to enjoy the curriculum, leading to them thinking of themselves as 'historians', 'geographers', 'scientists', etc. • The balance between practise and consolidation and providing opportunities for deep learning, especially for more able pupils, is most evident and providing a platform for developing scholastic excellence. • The teacher has been highly successful in getting a love for literature across to all learners, resulting in learners being able to engage with literature in a very positive and exciting way.

Strand 5

Differentiation

5.1   Is there evidence that those requiring intervention are being identified so that all learners keep up?

5.2   Is learning appropriately differentiated with evidence conclusive within different books?

5.3   Is there evidence that differentiation is achieved by emphasising deep knowledge and through individual support and intervention?

5.4   Is there evidence of deep learning, especially for more able learners?

Strand 5   Differentiation

5.1   Is there evidence that those requiring intervention are being identified so that all learners keep up?

Inadequate	Requires Improvement	Good	Outstanding
• It is evident that the tasks provided for lower attaining pupils do not match their requirements. There is a strong sense that the tasks provided for lower attaining pupils are of 'keeping them occupied' nature rather than helping to improve their skills. • There is no culture of creating 'pre-learning' activities so as to identify barriers to learning. This leads to activities being provided for lower attaining learners which do not lead to them 'catching up' with their peers.	• Learners who are finding it difficult to 'keep up' are provided with additional support as, and when, they need it. • There is a lack of a clear system that helps to identify what the barriers are to learning. Therefore most lower attaining learners have activities which do not match the expectations of their age group. • Too frequently lower attaining pupils have tasks which are very different to others in their class. • The quality of intervention is variable leading to progress being too slow for many requiring additional support.	• There is a well known and accepted system in place which identifies individuals requiring additional support. • There is a process in place that ensures that learners receiving intervention are able to access learning related to their own age group as soon as possible. • There is evidence that the learners receiving intervention change according to the needs identified in the pre learning activities as well as with on-going activities in the classroom.	• Pre learning checks are being used to help identify learners who require intervention. • The identification of different learners for different activities and tasks according to the outcomes from pre-learning and pre-teaching tasks is happening regularly. • Pupils are identified for pre-teaching. • The work in books of pupils in receipt of intervention shows that they are being supported well so as to access the tasks for their own age group as soon as is possible and practicable. • Evidence in books shows that the most able learners are given opportunities to access deeper learning & develop mastery in a range of contexts. • Evidence from learners books show that the teacher has excellent knowledge of the year group expectations across all subjects and is quick to identify exactly what needs to happen to provide additional support.

Strand 5   Differentiation

5.2   Is learning appropriately differentiated with evidence conclusive within different books?

Inadequate	Requires Improvement	Good	Outstanding
• The evidence in books suggest that too many learners have been asked to complete the same tasks, irrespective of ability. • Teaching and planning demonstrates a lack of knowledge or understanding of the learners' differing levels of attainment and learning needs. • The most able learners are not being challenged effectively. • Teaching strategies are limited in range and may be repetitive, having limited impact on learning for groups of learners. • Support and intervention strategies have limited impact on learning, and may actually hinder learners' progress.	• There is not enough evidence in books to suggest that activities have been varied enough to take full account of the differing abilities of the learners. • The teaching and planning takes some account of the differing levels of attainment and needs of the learners. • The most able learners are being challenged, but not consistently or across all subjects. • There are some different strategies being used to help groups of learners make progress more effectively. • A few support and intervention strategies have some impact over time.	• It is evident that teaching and planning demonstrates that teachers are well aware of the different levels of attainment in the class and they meet the needs of groups of pupils, including the most able, based on formative assessment information. • It is clear that teachers often use well-judged teaching strategies across a number of subjects. • It is evident that a range of teaching strategies are used to meet the needs of learners and these are evaluated and adapted over time. • It is clear that any support and intervention is well targeted and is matched closely to most learners' needs, including those most and least able, so that learners learn well in lessons.	• Evaluation of a range of books shows that teachers prepare a range of learning that takes full account of their knowledge of individual pupils and groups of pupils. • Teachers are happy to vary their groups according to the information gained from pre-learning activities. • Evidence shows that differentiation in all subjects takes full account of the principles that more able pupils should be challenged through more complex problem solving rather than on drawing from new learning from a higher age group. • Evidence shows that differentiation involves thinking more in depth rather than more difficult numbers.

Strand 5   Differentiation

5.3   Is there evidence that differentiation is achieved by emphasising deep knowledge and through individual support and intervention?

Inadequate	Requires Improvement	Good	Outstanding
• There is little or no evidence of the activities provided for more able learners helping to deepen their learning. • Tasks for more able tend to be extension activities. • Lower attainers are being provided with 'easier' work which in some cases contain far too much 'colouring in' or simple tasks that do not help to move on their learning. • Barriers to learning are not being identified in a systematic way and therefore the same group of learners are being labelled as 'lower attainers'.	• The activities provided for more able learners is not helping them to think more deeply. • Too frequently, more able learners are expected to do more and to work faster rather than to think more deeply and to work more smartly. • The intervention system is not helping to guarantee that lower attainers are being helped to access the learning designed for their age group. • There is a limited sense of the barriers to learning being identified for lower attaining pupils. • Differentiation across the class is far too varied and there seems to be a sense of rigid groups that are provided with different activities. • The quality of intervention provided is improving and beginning to ensure that learners can access the learning designed for their age group.	• There is evidence that more able learners are being provide with challenging tasks linked to the main learning. • Lower attaining learners are being provided with the appropriate level of support but expected to work to the activities for their age group. • The arrangements for identifying the barriers to learning are in place but as yet not fully impacting on learning. • There is a sense that activities for more able involves more in depth thinking but this is not fully established as yet.	• Evidence in books show that able learners have been provided with effective levels of challenge that take full account of their context and are helped to apply their knowledge across a broad range of subjects. • It is also evident that lower attaining learners are being provided with the right level of support to enable them to access the most appropriate learning for their age group. • A system of identification of barriers to learning is well established and used well to ensure that potentially vulnerable pupils are supported appropriately. • The quality of intervention provided for vulnerable learners impacts positively on pupils outcomes. • It is clear that differentiation for able learners involves thinking in more depth not just more difficult work.

Strand 5   Differentiation

5.4   Is there evidence of deep learning, especially for the most able?

Inadequate	Requires Improvement	Good	Outstanding
• There is little, if any, evidence of deep learning activities taking place. • More able learners are expected to work through the activities at a faster pace and no adjustment is made for the fact they have understood the concept and could be moved on to a deep learning activity.	• There is limited opportunity for pupils to be engaged in deep learning activities. • When provided with opportunities to think more deeply the activity is usually outside the context of the on-going learning taking place. • Too frequently the challenge for more able pupils is related to doing 'harder things' than having to think more deeply. • There is evidence that rather than deepening learning; content has been taken from the higher year group.	• Deep learning opportunities are being provided on a regular basis and there is clarity about it being a fundamental part of learning for more able pupils in particular. • The application of reading, writing, mathematical and ICT skills across the curriculum is something that is happening regularly. • The principles of deep learning are not always evident on a lesson-by-lesson basis in order to challenge more able pupils' thinking at a consistent level. • Learners clearly enjoy being challenged, especially when the deep learning activity is set in context.	• There are excellent examples of learners applying logic and reasoning to solve problems. • There is consistent evidence of learners applying their reading, writing, mathematical and ICT skills exceptionally skilfully in all of their learning, leading to their research skills being particularly good. • Challenge for more able pupils comes from them having to think more deeply about the concept or topic being taught. • It is clear that fluency, including conceptual understanding, reasoning mathematically and problem solving, are very important and are integral to the teaching taking place.

Strand 6

Progress

6.1   Is there evidence that pupils' understanding during a lesson is being systematically checked and adjustments made as needed?

6.2   Are there procedures in place to help learners know exactly what they need to achieve?

6.3   Is there conclusive evidence of pupils demonstrating sufficient gains in knowledge, skills and understanding?

6.4   Has progress been rapid enough from the beginning of the year; and last half term to the present day?

Strand 6   Progress

6.1   Is there evidence that pupils' understanding during a lesson is being systematically checked and adjustments made as needed?

Inadequate	Requires Improvement	Good	Outstanding
• There is no evidence of learners' work being checked leading to adjustments in the learning taking place. • The purpose of the learning is not well known to individual learners. • Teachers are not helping learners to know how well they are achieving and what goals they are working towards. • Teachers have not helped learners to explain how success criteria could be used to support their learning. • Teachers have not helped learners to know how to use feedback from others to make improvements.	• There are occasional examples of the teacher identifying errors in learners' work and making adjustments to the learning taking place. • Knowledge of the learning is used reasonably well to help individuals to make progress. • Learners work does not show evidence of the teacher using success criteria appropriately to evaluate learning. • Teachers do not make use of feedback from others to help make improvements in learners' work.	• There are many examples where the teacher has identified errors in learners' work and has therefore provided additional tasks to help to secure understanding. • There is good evidence that previous learning is very well linked to new learning, leading to much improved progress. • Teaching has clearly helped learners know why they are learning what they are, based on previous learning. • Success criteria are routinely used as a way to check progress by both pupils and teachers. • It is evident from feedback that learners know what they need to do in order to maintain high rates of learning.	• There are numerous examples where the teacher has consistently identified errors in learners' work and has therefore provided additional tasks to help to secure understanding. • The link between previous learning and new learning has clearly been made explicit to different groups of learners taking account of aptitude and ability. • There is evidence that learners are fully involved in defining success criteria and using them effectively to evaluate learning and set new goals. • There is evidence that learners have been provided with time to review progress and action-plan next steps based on their own evaluations and feedback from others.

Strand 6 Progress

6.2 Are there procedures in place to help learners know exactly what they need to achieve?

Inadequate	Requires Improvement	Good	Outstanding
• It is rare that targets or success criteria are being identified and promoted. • From the evidence it is apparent that learners do not know what they need to do in order to either accelerate their learning or to improve the standard of their work. • Progress is too slow because there is not system in place to help them identify barriers to their learning; or to identify what they need to do next.	• Although learners have targets, they tend to generic in nature and not specific enough to help learners improve at the rate they need to. • There is insufficient evidence that there is any reference being made to the targets, either as part of the on-going learning in the feedback learners receive. • There is insufficient evidence that deeper analysis of each learner is happening and leading to clear identification of what needs to happen in able for them to improve. The identification of the next steps for learning is inconsistent.	• Good use is made of such strategies as learning logs and success criteria, to help learners recognise how much progress they have made in the short and medium term. • It is evident that learners know their targets and they are contributing greatly to making a difference to the standard of their work. • Targets set out in books are child-friendly and help learners understand what it is they need to do next to improve. • It is clear that the teacher effectively evaluates performance and plans for progress from the information gathered about individual learner's success with targets.	• Excellent self-assessment systems have been established that help learners to make outstanding progress. • It is evident that learners can evaluate their progress against the targets they have. They are making secure judgements in relation to how successful they are in meeting these targets. • It is evident that learners are the instigators of the setting and reviewing of learning targets in both core and foundations subjects. • Learners are encouraged to use a range of resources for setting, recording and reviewing targets, and respond constructively to feedback provided. • Targets are organised around age group expectations with a clear view to lift achievement. • In mathematics, learners can set targets from clear information about what they should achieve on an annual basis.

Strand 6   Progress

6.3   Is there conclusive evidence of pupils demonstrating sufficient gains in knowledge, skills and understanding?

Inadequate	Requires Improvement	Good	Outstanding
• There is a lack of purpose to the learning taking place which leads to gains in knowledge, skills and understanding being far too slow. • Far too many activities do not directly link to the year group expectations of the pupils. • There is sense that the teacher does not have clarity about the year group expectations and the journey that the pupils are making towards them. The progress of more able learners is being slowed down because they are not being provided with deep learning opportunities.	• The rate of progress made, as seen in learners books, is variable. • Too many learners are not on track to meet the year group expectations because the pace of learning has not been demanding enough. • Although the learning undertaken directly relates to the year group expectations, too much time has been taken up with activities which will not ensure that learners are in a good position to meet the year group expectations. • Learners lack confidence in many aspects of their learning which leads to a negative impact on their knowledge, skills and understanding. • There is insufficient evidence of English and mathematics skills being used across the curriculum.	• It is evident that individuals are making progress at a good rate. • There is good evidence that learners are sufficiently motivated to carry on learning beyond the classroom. • It is clear that the majority of the class is on course to meet the age expectations for their year by the end of the academic year. • Learners have confidence in communicating their understanding when it is related to English or mathematical activities. • Although the evidence is conclusive that they make progress in writing, reading and mathematics it less conclusive when it comes to other subjects or the application of writing, reading and mathematics skills across the curriculum.	• It is evident that learners are making excellent gains in their knowledge, skills and understanding across all subjects. • Pupils apply age-appropriate literacy and numeracy skills in all aspects of their work with confidence. • Learners successfully communicate their understanding in a range of different ways having excellent consideration for the audience. • Learners show capability of explaining their knowledge and link what has come before with what might come after. • Where appropriate, the teacher has provided opportunities for learners to deepen their learning. • There are examples of learners choosing to continue to learn at school and beyond using appropriate resources in depth to deepen learning. • The teacher provides opportunities for learners to reflect critically on strengths and weaknesses and be involved in choosing tasks which address any weaknesses.

Strand 6   Progress

6.4   Has progress been rapid enough from the beginning of the year; and last half term to the present day?

Inadequate	Requires Improvement	Good	Outstanding
• The evidence is conclusive that far too little progress has been made between September and the last piece of work produced across most subjects. The quality of written work has not improved sufficiently to give confidence that progress has been as expected let alone good. • In some cases, there is evidence that pupils' learning has gone backwards. • There is little evidence of learners applying their knowledge, skills and understanding in reading, writing and mathematics across the curriculum, leading to outcomes in other subjects being poor.	• The evidence is inconclusive that learners are making sufficient gains in their knowledge, skills and understanding at a rapid enough rate. The gains made in reading, writing and mathematics are not being translated across the rest of the curriculum. When analysing the learning done in September there is not evidence that learners' knowledge, skills and understanding in such aspects as writing, especially use of grammar and number have improved at the rate expected. • There are few, if any, deep learning examples which gives confidence that learners are mastering the expectations for their age group.	• Overall, there is a good sense of improvement having happened between September and the latest work produced. The evidence shows that learners have made improvement in key areas such as ability to use grammar; spelling; sentence structure, number, geometry and measurement. • The evidence of improvement across the curriculum is less secure. • There are good examples of deep learning opportunities being provided for learners, which indicates that they are mastering the knowledge, skills and understanding for their age.	• There is conclusive evidence that there has been vast improvement in learners' outcomes when looking at what was being produced at the beginning of the year and their latest work. • The improvement goes beyond just presentation. There is evidence of improvement in the quality of work which can be evidenced in improvement in their journey towards being at the national standard and towards mastery, where applicable. The balance of the work undertaken by the pupils shows that there is sufficient intervention being given when needed and deep learning opportunities being provided when necessary. • When looking at the first tasks undertaken in September, compared with the latest work, there is conclusive evidence that the learners are able to do things now that they could not have done in September.

This is an early example of work from a Year 5 pupil in September.

Wednesday 17ᵗʰ September 2014   ① I have talked to my partner
Can I add my imagination?   for more of ideas.

Teacher annotations (in red):

Use speech marks (inverted commas) when someone is speaking
eg. "Stop!" shouted the policeman.

What is missing from this word? ←——— black

I will not keep reminding you about this!
Black
ed/endings ✓ yes.

Pupil text:

Planet Robo is a colossal ③ is a bumpy planet with a squmbish of jet black? pebbles. Everything is frosty ④ my grumps turbines he only fly that lives. There are robots with right houses. It is two two hundred million kilometers away from Earth. The colors are multicolored multicolored ecator because of the inside of the planet. You always hear clanging ① sounds around you. When ever you walk your feet made a clang sound. I nearly forgot that the houses can walk and make runs ⑩ my sulfia of Planet Robo is smoky and rut. cough

sp.

Thursday 5ᵗʰ February 2016

Can I use the glues of a flashback?

Kidnapped 1

Someone was walking down the stairs. My nans groaned like crazy. Sneaking down behind an old rusty container we couldn't see... the strange girl had red straight hair and dark brown hair. What if we were caught? All of a sudden we heard a b... go back to... the stairs. The strange girl, white's eyes... gleamed, smiled. (whuh sh... felt terrified).

Shortly the door opened and a light flickered on. The lights beam... off the torch a darkness. Sneaking up... out the kidnappers gradually flicked off the torch a... lift the room. However we could hear a persons voice echoing down the narrow hall. Then foot steps clicked down the stairs. Relived I let out a sigh. How... could I get into this mess? Trying to remember we stumbled out of the com... slowly contemplate.

It... Suddenly the power went off. I was on my way to the electronic shop. [long] (O) had only been a short while ago when I was happily playing gui... saw a girl waving from a window. I was in an abandon power plant. ... stuck in from a damaged door at the back.

That's how I got into the mess 5 minutes later I found a fisherman (or a room on the mid floor). She said "I'm famous sing a Elly's sister, Elly." Just as the kidnappers came back.

We slid down the largest and held back to my house. "Where have you be all day." asked my mum.

Ishaq

Can I write my own flashback story?	Me	Peer Assess
Problem – present tense, first person.		✓
Flashback – past tense		
Include senses and emotions touch; see, hear, smell, feel		✓
Adverbial openers – link events time and place		✓
Range of punctuation – " " : ; , … ( ) . ? !		✓
Powerful verbs, adverbs, descriptive phrases		✓
Different sentence types		
Similes, metaphors		

☆ I like your Punctuation (excellent) ": ? "
✓ Improv Improve your metaphors

* Question sentence
* Short sentence
* E.V.Y.S.
* Panel...
* ...

This is the same learner's work in February. This clearly evidences progress over time.

6.4 Outstanding

The improvement goes beyond just presentation. There is evidence of improvement in the quality of work which can be evidenced in improvement in their journey towards being at the national standard and towards mastery

Two examples of writing from a Reception aged learner

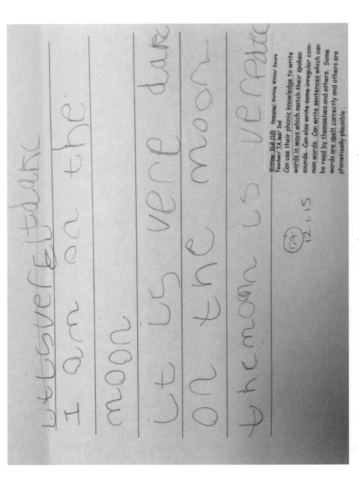

Reece in March

This evidences progress over time.

6.4 Outstanding

There is conclusive evidence that there has been vast improvement in learners' outcomes when looking at what was being produced at the beginning of the year and their latest work.

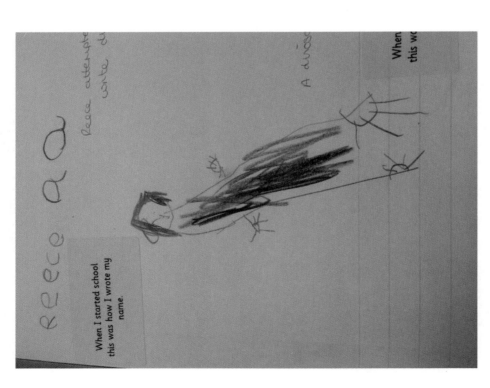

Reece in September

Year 1 September

Focus Es Es for
forup Cofsee
fun grana
h ut pouyern

Year 1 February

They told us lots of things in the firengine. We went inside the fireman altoth then wt was dresso got. Like a helmat. Martin showed us now he looked like in his cloaths with a helmet and a breathing apparatws. what question could you ask a fireman? How many fire's do you blast off?

An example of one pupil's improvement between September and February.

When looking at the first tasks undertaken in September, compared with the latest work, there is conclusive evidence that the learners are able to do things now that they could not have done in September.

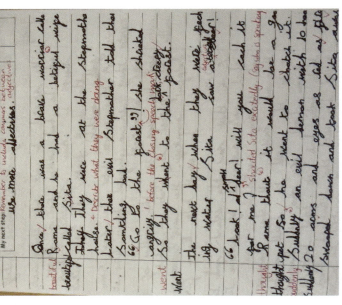

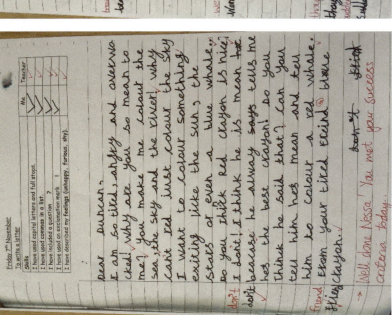

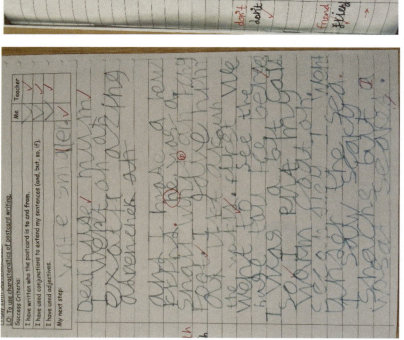

Here is an example of the same Year 2 learners writing between September and February. The first is in September; the second November and the third is February.

6.4 Outstanding

When looking at the first tasks undertaken in September, compared with the latest work, there is conclusive evidence that the learners are able to do things now that they could not have done in September.

© Focus Education UK Ltd. 2015

54

Strand 7

Appropriate Praise

7.1 Is there evidence of a climate being created where pupils' learning, in the form of finished outcomes, is really valued?

7.2 Is there evidence that learners' successes are being 'celebrated'?

Strand 7   Appropriate Praise

7.1   Is there evidence of a climate being created where pupils' learning, in the form of finished outcomes, is really valued?

Inadequate	Requires Improvement	Good	Outstanding
• There is little pride taken in the finished outcomes. • Work can often be shoddy and incomplete and can vary greatly from day to day. • There is little sense that learners have been provided with clarity about what was expected of them. • Much of the work in the foundation subjects is of a poor quality. • Too frequently, it is clear that learners have not been asked to check through their finished outcomes, leading to too many mistakes which could have been dealt with.	• Finished outcomes tend to be variable with examples of both good and indifferent work being evident. • Although learners take a pride in their finished work this is not always the case across all the class. • The standard of work in foundation subjects is often not of the same quality of that of core subjects. • Work on display is of a varied quality and is often put up without a context and not named, which does not help to create a sense of celebrating the outcomes. • Praise tends to be for the work produced with little attention given to how hard someone has worked.	• Learners clearly take pride in their achievements, despite the fact that this is sometimes measured in neatness rather than quality of outcomes. • It is clear that learners are striving to do their best. • Learners show off their books with pride and are keen to engage the listener in what they have done. • Not all outcomes are in written formats and there is good evidence of finished outcomes across several subjects. • There is evidence of finished outcomes on display in the classroom and in shared areas. • Work displayed is of a high standard, with care taken to present it well.	• It is very clear that learners take a great deal of pride in their work and they strive to achieve well. • The written dialogue that exists between the teacher and the learners gives every indication that there is mutual respect between teacher and learner. • Learners know where they stand and take an enormous amount of pride in their finished outcomes. • There is an excellent range of outcomes available which also includes IT driven outcomes. • Beyond what is in the books, there is evidence, through displays, that learners' work is being highly valued. • The school has a system in place of regularly celebrating learners' outcomes and this extends to using the website and involving parents directly. • Appropriate praise is given for working hard.

Strand 7   Appropriate Praise

7.2   Is there evidence that learners' successes are being 'celebrated'?

Inadequate	Requires Improvement	Good	Outstanding
• There is little evidence of any praise being given. However, there is evidence of individuals being picked up for what they have not done well or for when they have not tried hard enough. • The lack of balance between praise and criticism leads to a lack of motivation. • On the odd occasion praise is given it lacks any sense of belonging to an individual and can be too generic.	• There is a sense of praise being more to do with being clever than for genuinely working hard. • Praise is often inconsistent and too frequently out of context. • Although praise is a regular part of feedback and marking, it seems to do little to spur individuals on to greater achievement. • The praise given can too often be remarks such as 'well done' without any further reference as to what the learner has done well. • Praise tends not to be valued by individuals as it lacks sincerity.	• Praise is a frequently used strategy to further motivate individuals. • There is a good sense of consistency associated with the praise given. • Individuals clearly value the praise that is given to them. • Praise tends to be given within context and is not over-lavish. • There is more focus on praising for hard work than for being clever. • On the whole, praise is effective but it can be a little inconsistent at times. • There is care taken that the praise is clearly linked to individual pupils.	• Praise is given regularly, appropriately and in context. • The praise given is personalised and does not resort to 'generic' terms, as a result the praise has a strong sense of sincerity associated with it. • Teachers use the learner's name positively to ensure that the praise comes across as being particular to that one learner. • Teachers avoid any temptation to 'over-praise' and therefore, when given, the praise is highly valued by individuals. • It is evident that learners are not praised for being clever when they succeed at something, but instead are praised for working hard. • It is evident that it is hard work that is consistently being praised and not just ability or output.

Making Book Scrutiny More Meaningful

Linking Book Scrutiny to Teaching Judgements

Part Two:

What does being at the National Standard look like in relation to different year groups?

What does being at National Expectation look like in relation to different year groups?

The next few pages set out the National Expectations against each age group in writing, mathematics and science.

- What is set out are the key assessment criteria. In other words if the learners are doing these you can be satisfied that they are 'at the National Standard' for their age.

- Naturally, all the statements from this section are drawn directly from the National Curriculum.

- These key criteria do not include every element of the national curriculum but are presented as a summary to help gain an overview of the standard being evidenced in a child's book.

At Mastery level, learners need to show that they can deal with the expectations independently, fluently and use their reasoning skills. The main elements are set out below.	
Independence	Can apply the skill or knowledge without recall to the teacher.
Fluency	Can apply the skill and knowledge with a high level of confidence.
Application	Can apply the skill and knowledge to a range of different contexts, including other areas of the curriculum.
Consistency	Will be consistent in their use of the skills and knowledge
Synthesise	Can organise ideas, information, or experiences into new, more complex interpretations and relationships;
Re-visit	Can come back to this aspect of learning after a break and still feel confident that they can work on the skill and knowledge without difficulty.

What does being at the National Standard look like in relation to different year groups?

Writing

Writing
By the end of Year 1 learners should be able to:

A year 1 writer

Transcription

Spelling

- Identify known phonemes in unfamiliar words.
- Use syllables to divide words when spelling.
- Use what is known about alternative phonemes to narrow down possibilities for accurate spelling.
- Use the spelling rule for adding 's' or 'es' for verbs in the 3rd person singular.
- Name all the letters of the alphabet in order.
- Use letter names to show alternative spellings of the same phoneme.

Handwriting

- Sit correctly at a table, holding a pencil comfortable and correctly.
- Form lower case letters in the correct direction, starting and finishing in the right place.
- Form capital letters and digits 0-9.

Composition

- Compose a sentence orally before writing it.
- Sequence sentences in chronological order to recount and event or experience.
- Re-read what I have written to check that it makes sense.
- Leave spaces between words.
- Know how the prefix 'un' can be added to words to change meaning.
- Use the suffixes 's', 'es', 'ed', and 'ing' within my writing.

Grammar and punctuation

Sentence structure

- Combine words to make a sentence.
- Join two sentences using 'and'.

Text structure

- Sequence sentences to form a narrative.

Punctuation

- Separate words using finger spaces.
- Use capital letters to start a sentence.
- Use a full stop to end a sentence.
- Use a question mark.
- Use an exclamation mark.
- Use capital letters for names.
- Use 'I'.

Writing

By the end of Year 2 learners should be able to:

A year 2 writer

Transcription	Composition	Grammar and punctuation
Spelling	• Write narratives about personal experiences and those of others, both real and fictional.	**Sentence structure**
• Segment spoken words into phonemes and record these as graphemes.	• Write for different purposes, including real events.	• Use subordination and co-ordination.
• Spell words with alternatives spellings, including a few common homophones.	• Plan and discuss the content of writing and record my ideas.	• Use expanded noun phrases.
• Spell longer words using suffixes such as 'ment', 'ness', 'ful', 'less', 'ly'.	• Orally rehearse structured sentences or sequences of sentences.	• Say how the grammatical patterns in a sentence indicate its function.
• Use knowledge of alternative phonemes to narrow down possibilities for accurate spelling.	• Evaluate own writing independently, with friends and with an adult.	**Text structure**
• Identify phonemes in unfamiliar words and use syllables to divide words.	• Proof-read to check for errors in spelling, grammar and punctuation.	• Consistently use the present tense and past tense correctly.
Handwriting		• Use the progressive forms of verbs in the present and past tense.
• Form lower-case letters of the correct size relative to one another.		**Punctuation**
• Begin to use some of the diagonal and horizontal strokes needed to join letters.		• Use capital letters for names of people, places, day of the week and the personal pronoun 'I'.
• Know which letters are best not joined.		• Use question marks and exclamation marks.
• Use capital letters and digits of the correct size, orientation and relationship to one another and to lower case letters.		• Use commas to separate items in a list.
• Use spacing between words that reflects the size of the letters.		• Use apostrophes to show where letters are missing and to mark singular possession in nouns.

Writing
By the end of Year 3 learners should be able to:

A year 3 writer	
Transcription	**Composition**
Spelling	• Discuss models of writing, noting its structure, grammatical features and use of vocabulary.
• Spell words with additional prefixes and suffixes and understand how to add them to root words.	• Compose sentences using a wider range of structures.
• Recognise and spell homophones.	• Write a narrative with a clear structure, setting, characters and plot.
• Use the first two or three letters of a word to check its spelling in a dictionary.	• Write non-narrative using simple organisational devices such as headings and sub-headings.
• Spell words correctly which are in a family.	• Suggest improvements to my own writing and that of others.
• Spell the commonly mis-spelt words from the Y3/4 word list.	• Make improvements to grammar, vocabulary and punctuation.
• Identify the root in longer words.	• Use a range of sentences with more than one clause by using a range of conjunctions.
Handwriting	• Use the perfect form of verbs to mark the relationship of time and cause.
• Use the diagonal and horizontal strokes that are needed to join letters.	• Proof-read to check for errors in spelling and punctuation.
• Understand which letters should be left unjoined.	

Grammar and punctuation
Sentence structure
• Express time, place and cause by using conjunctions, adverbs and prepositions.
Text structure
• Starting to use paragraphs.
• Use headings and sub headings.
• Use the present perfect form of verbs instead of the simple past.
Punctuation
• Use inverted commas to punctuate direct speech.

Writing

By the end of Year 4 learners should be able to:

A year 4 writer

Transcription	Composition	Grammar and punctuation
Spelling • Spell words with prefixes and suffixes and can add them to root words. • Recognise and spell homophones. • Use the first two or three letters of a word to check a spelling in a dictionary. • Spell the commonly mis-spelt words from the Y3/4 word list. **Handwriting** • Use the diagonal and horizontal strokes that are needed to join letters. • Understand which letters should be left unjoined. • Handwriting is legible and consistent; down strokes of letters are parallel and equidistant; lines of writing are spaced sufficiently so that ascenders and descenders of letters do not touch.	• Compose sentences using a range of sentence structures. • Orally rehearse a sentence or a sequence of sentences. • Write a narrative with a clear structure, setting and plot. • Improve my writing by changing grammar and vocabulary to improve consistency. • Use a range of sentences which have more than one clause. • Use appropriate nouns and pronouns within and across sentences to support cohesion and avoid repetition. • Use direct speech in my writing and punctuate it correctly.	**Sentence structure** • Use noun phrases which are expanded by adding modifying adjectives, nouns and preposition phrases. • Use fronted adverbials. **Text structure** • Write in paragraphs. • Make an appropriate choice of pronoun and noun within and across sentences. **Punctuation** • Use inverted commas and other punctuation to indicate direct speech. • Use apostrophes to mark plural possession. • Use commas after fronted adverbials.

Writing
By the end of Year 5 learners should be able to:

A year 5 writer		
Transcription	**Composition**	**Grammar and punctuation**
Spelling	• Discuss the audience and purpose of the writing.	Sentence structure
• Form verbs with prefixes.	• Start sentences in different ways.	• Use relative clauses.
• Convert nouns or adjectives into verbs by adding a suffix.	• Use the correct features and sentence structure matched to the text type we are working on.	• Use adverbs or modal verbs to indicate a degree of possibility.
• Understand the rules for adding prefixes and suffixes.	• Develop characters through action and dialogue.	Text structure
• Spell words with silent letters.	• Establish a viewpoint as the writer through commenting on characters and events.	• Build cohesion between paragraphs.
• Distinguish between homophones and other words which are often confused.	• Use grammar and vocabulary to create an impact on the reader.	• Use adverbials to link paragraphs.
• Spell the commonly mis-spelt words from the Y5/6 word list.	• Use stylistic devices to create effects in writing.	Punctuation
• Use the first 3 or 4 letters of a word to check spelling, meaning or both in a dictionary.	• Add well chosen detail to interest the reader.	• Use brackets, dashes and commas to indicate parenthesis.
• Use a thesaurus.	• Summarise a paragraph.	• Use commas to clarify meaning or avoid ambiguity.
• Use a range of spelling strategies.	• Organise my writing into paragraphs to show different information or events.	
Handwriting		
• Choose the style of handwriting to use when given a choice.		
• Choose the handwriting that is best suited for a specific task.		

Writing

By the end of Year 6 learners should be able to:

A year 6 writer		
Transcription	**Composition**	**Grammar and punctuation**
Spelling	• Identify the audience for and purpose of the writing.	Sentence structure
• Convert verbs into nouns by adding a suffix.	• Choose the appropriate form and register for the audience and purpose of the writing.	• Use the passive voice.
• Distinguish between homophones and other words which are often confused.	• Use grammatical structures and features and choose vocabulary appropriate to the audience, purpose and degree of formality to make meaning clear and create effect.	• Vary sentence structure depending whether formal or informal.
• Spell the commonly mis-spelt words from the Y5/6 word list.		Text structure
• Understand that the spelling of some words need to be learnt specifically.	• Use a range of sentence starters to create specific effects.	• Use a variety of organisational and presentational devices correct to the text type.
• Use any dictionary or thesaurus.	• Use developed noun phrases to add detail to sentences.	• Write in paragraphs which can clearly signal a change in subject, time, place or event.
• Use a range of spelling strategies.	• Use the passive voice to present information with a different emphasis.	Punctuation
Handwriting	• Use commas to mark phrases and clauses.	• Use the semi-colon, colon and dash.
• Choose the style of handwriting to use when given a choice.	• Sustain and develop ideas logically in narrative and non-narrative writing.	• Use the colon to introduce a list and semi-colon within lists.
• Choose the handwriting that is best suited for a specific task.	• Use character, dialogue and action to advance events in narrative writing.	• Use a hyphen to avoid ambiguity.
	• Summarise a text, conveying key information in writing.	

What does being at the National Standard look like in relation to different year groups?

Mathematics

Mathematics
By the end of Year 1 - learners should be able to:

A year 1 Mathematician	Measurement and geometry
Number	
• Count reliably to 100.	• Recognise all coins.
• Count on and back in 1s, 2s, 5s and 10s from any given number up to 100.	• Recognise and can name the 2D shapes: circle, triangle, square and rectangle.
• Write all numbers in words to 20.	• Recognise and can name the 3D shapes: cuboid, pyramid, sphere.
• Day the number that is one more or one less than a number to 100.	• Name the days of the week and months of the year.
• Recall all pairs of addition and subtraction number bonds to 20.	• Tell the time to o'clock and half past the hour.
• Add and subtract 1-digit and 2-digit numbers to 20, including zero.	
• Know the signs + - =.	
• Solve a missing number problem.	
• Solve a one-step problem using addition and subtraction, using concrete objects and pictorial representations.	

Mathematics

By the end of Year 2 - learners should be able to:

A year 2 Mathematician

Number

- Read and write all numbers to at least 100 in numerals and words.

- Recognise odd and even numbers to 100.

- Count in steps of 2, 3 and 5 from 0.

- Recognise and can define the place value of each digit in a 2 digit number.

- Compare and order numbers from 0 to 100 using the < > and = signs.

- Name the fractions 1/3, 1/4, 1/2 and 3/4 and can find fractional values of shapes, lengths and numbers.

- Recall and use multiplication and division facts for the 2, 5 and 10x tables.

- Add and subtract a 2-digit number and ones.

- Add and subtract a 2-digit number and tens.

- Add and subtract two 2-digit numbers.

- Add three 1-digit numbers.

- Solve problems involving addition and subtraction.

- Understand and can use commutivity in relation to addition, subtraction, multiplication and division.

Measurement, geometry and statistics

- Choose and use appropriate standard units to estimate length, height, temperature and capacity.

- Tell and write the time to 5 minute intervals.

- Recognise and can use the symbols £ and p when solving problems involving addition and subtraction of money.

- Describe the properties of 2D and 3D shapes to include edges, vertices and faces.

- Interpret and construct pictograms, tally charts, block diagram and simple tables.

Mathematics
By the end of Year 3 - learners should be able to:

A year 3 Mathematician

Number

- Compare and order numbers to 1000 and read and write numbers to 1000 in numerals and words.

- Count from 0 in multiples of 4, 8, 50 and 100.

- Recognise the value of each digit in a 3-digit number.

- Understand and can count in tenths, and find the fractional value of a given set.

- Add and subtract fractions with a common denominator.

- Derive and recall multiplication facts for 3, 4 and 8x tables.

- Add and subtract mentally combinations of 1-digit and 2-digit numbers.

- Add and subtract numbers with up to 3-digits using formal written methods.

- Write and calculate mathematical statements for multiplication and vision using the 2x, 3x, 4x, 5x, 8x and 10x tables.

- Calculate 2-digit x 1-digit.

- Solve number problems using one and two step problems

Measurement, geometry and statistics

- Identify right angles and can compare other angles stating whether they are greater or smaller than a right angle.

- Identify horizontal and vertical lines and pairs of perpendicular and parallel lines.

- Tell the time to the nearest minute and use specific vocabulary, including seconds, am & pm.

- Measure, compare, add and subtract using common metric measures.

- Solve one and two step problems using information presented in scaled bar charts, pictograms and tables.

Mathematics

By the end of Year 4 - learners should be able to:

A year 4 Mathematician

Number

- Recall all multiplication facts to 12 x 12.

- Round any number to the nearest 10, 100 or 1000 and decimals with one decimal place to the nearest whole number.

- Count backwards through zero to include negative numbers.

- Compare numbers with the same number of decimal places up to 2-decimal places.

- Recognise and write decimal equivalents of any number of tenths or hundredths.

- Add and subtract with up to 4-decimal places using formal written methods of columnar addition and subtraction.

- Divide a 1 or 2-digit number by 10 or 100 identifying the value of the digits in the answer as units, tenths and hundredths.

- Multiply 2-digit and 3-digit numbers by a 1-digit number using formal written layout.

- Solve two step addition and subtraction problems in context.

- Solve problems involving multiplication.

Measurement, geometry and statistics

- Compare and classify geometrical shapes, including quadrilaterals and triangles, based on their properties and sizes.

- Know that angles are measured in degrees and can identify acute and obtuse angles.

- Compare and order angles up to two right angles by size.

- Measure and calculate the perimeter of a rectilinear figure in cm and m.

- Read, write and convert between analogue and digital 12 and 24 hour times.

- Interpret and present discrete and continuous data using appropriate graphical methods, including bar charts and time graphs.

Mathematics

By the end of Year 5 - learners should be able to:

A year 5 Mathematician

Number

- Count forwards and backwards in steps of powers of 10 for any given number up to 1,000,000.

- Recognise and use thousandths and relate then to tenths, hundredths and decimals equivalents.

- Recognise mixed numbers and improper fractions and can convert from one to the other.

- Read and write decimal numbers as fractions.

- Recognise the % symbol and understand percent relates to a number of parts per hundred.

- Write percentages as a fraction with denominator hundred and as a decimal fraction.

- Compare and add fractions whose denominators are all multiples of the same number.

- Multiply and divide numbers mentally drawing on known facts up to 12 x 12.

- Round decimals with 2dp to the nearest whole number and to 1dp.

- Recognise and use square numbers and cube numbers; and can use the notation ^{2} and ^{3}.

- Multiply and divide whole numbers and those involving decimals by 10, 100 and 1000.

- Multiply numbers up to 4-digit by a 1 or 2-digit number using formal written methods, including long multiplication for a 2-digit number.

- Divide numbers up to 4-digits by a 1-digit number.

- Solve problems involving multiplication and division where large numbers are used by decomposing them into factors.

- Solve addition and subtraction multi-step problems in context, deciding which operations and methods to use and why.

- Solve problems involving numbers up to 3dp.

Measurement, geometry and statistics

- Know that angles are measured in degrees.

- Estimate and compare acute, obtuse and reflex angles.

- Draw given angles and measure them in degrees.

- Convert between different units of metric measures and estimate volume and capacity.

- Measure and calculate the perimeter of composite rectilinear shapes in cm and m.

- Calculate and compare the areas of squares and rectangles including using standards units (cm^2 and m^2).

- Solve comparison, sum and difference problems using information presented in a line graph.

Mathematics

By the end of Year 6 - learners should be able to:

A year 6 Mathematician

Number

- Use negative numbers in context, and calculate intervals across zero.
- Round any whole number to a required degree of accuracy and solve problems which require answers to be rounded to a specific degree of accuracy.
- Solve problems involving the relative sizes of two quantities where the missing values can be found by using integer multiplication and division facts.
- Use common factors to simplify fractions; use common multiples to express fractions in the same denomination.
- Solve problems involving the calculation of percentages.
- Multiply 1-digit numbers with up to two decimal places by whole numbers.
- Perform mental calculations, including with mixed operations with large numbers.
- Divide numbers up to 4-digits by a 2-digit whole number using formal written methods of long division and interpret remainder in various ways.
- Use knowledge of order of operations to carry out calculations involving all four operations.
- Add and subtract fractions with different denominators and mixed numbers, using the concept of equivalent fractions.
- Multiply simple pairs of proper fractions, writing the answer in its simplest form.
- Divide proper fractions by whole numbers.
- Associate a fraction with division and calculate decimal fraction equivalents.
- Express missing number problems algebraically.
- Find pairs of numbers that satisfy number sentences involving two unknowns.

Measurement, geometry and statistics

- Recognise, describe and build simple 3D shapes, including making nets.
- Compare and classify geometric shapes based on their properties and sizes and find unknown angles in any triangle, quadrilateral and regular polygons.
- Illustrate and name parts of circles, including radius, diameter and circumference and know that the radius is half the diameter.
- Read, write and convert between standard units, converting measurements of length, mass, volume and time from a smaller unit of measure to a larger unit, and visa versa, using decimal notation to up to 3 decimal places.
- Calculate the area of a parallelogram and triangles and calculate, estimate and compare volume of cubes and cuboids using standard units.
- Interpret and construct pie charts and line graphs and use these to solve problems.

What does being at the National Standard look like in relation to different year groups?

Science

Science

By the end of Year 1 - learners should be able to:

A year 1 scientist		
Working scientifically (Y1 and Y2)	**Biology**	**Chemistry**
• Ask simple scientific questions. • Use simple equipment to make observations. • Carry out simple tests. • Identify and classify things. • Suggest what has been found out. • Use simple data to answer questions.	Plants • Name a variety of common wild and garden plants. • Name the petals, stem, leaf and root of a plant. • Name the roots, trunk, branches and leaves of a tree. Animals, including humans • Name a variety of animals including fish, amphibians, reptiles birds and mammals. • Classify and name animals by what they eat (carnivore, herbivore and omnivore). • Sort animals into categories (including fish, amphibians, reptiles, birds and mammals). • Sort living and non-living things. • Name the parts of the human body that I can see. • Link the correct part of the human body to each sense.	Everyday materials • Distinguish between an object and the material it is made from. • Explain the materials that an object is made from. • Name wood, plastic, glass, metal, water and rock. • Describe the properties of everyday materials. • Group objects based on the materials they are made from.
		Physics
		Seasonal changes • Observe and comment on changes in the seasons. • Name the seasons and suggest the type of weather in each season.

Science

By the end of Year 2 - learners should be able to:

A year 2 scientist		
Working scientifically (Y1 and Y2)	**Biology**	**Chemistry**
• Ask simple scientific questions.	**Living things and their habitats**	**Uses of everyday materials**
• Use simple equipment to make observations.	• Identify things that are living, dead and never lived.	• Identify and name a range of materials, including wood, metal, plastic, glass, brick, rock, paper and cardboard.
• Carry out simple tests.	• Describe how a specific habitat provides for the basic needs of things living there (plants and animals).	• Suggest why a material might or might not be used for a specific job.
• Identify and classify things.	• Identify and name plants and animals in a range of habitats.	• Explore how shapes can be changed by squashing, bending, twisting and stretching.
• Suggest what has been found out.	• Match living things to their habitat.	
• Use simple data to answer questions.	• Describe how animals find their food.	
	• Name some different sources of food for animals.	
	• Explain a simple food chain.	
	Plants	
	• Describe how seeds and bulbs grow into plants.	
	• Describe what plants need in order to grow and stay healthy (water, light & suitable temperature).	
	Animals, including humans	**Physics**
	• Explain the basic stages in a life cycle for animals, including humans.	No content
	• Describe what animals and humans need to survive.	
	• Describe why exercise, a balanced diet and good hygiene are important for humans.	

Science

By the end of Year 3 - learners should be able to:

A year 3 scientist

Working scientifically (Y3 and Y4)

- Ask relevant scientific questions.
- Use observations and knowledge to answer scientific questions.
- Set up a simple enquiry to explore a scientific question.
- Set up a test to compare two things.
- Set up a fair test and explain why it is fair.
- Make careful and accurate observations, including the use of standard units.
- Use equipment, including thermometers and data loggers to make measurements.
- Gather, record, classify and present data in different ways to answer scientific questions.
- Use diagrams, keys, bar charts and tables; using scientific language.
- Use findings to report in different ways, including oral and written explanations, presentation.
- Draw conclusions and suggest improvements.
- Make a prediction with a reason.
- Identify differences, similarities and changes related to an enquiry.

Biology

Plants

- Describe the function of different parts of flowing plants and trees.
- Explore and describe the needs of different plants for survival.
- Explore and describe how water is transported within plants.
- Describe the plant life cycle, especially the importance of flowers.

Animals, including humans

- Explain the importance of a nutritious, balanced diet.
- Explain how nutrients, water and oxygen are transported within animals and humans.
- Describe and explain the skeletal system of a human.
- Describe and explain the muscular system of a human.
- Describe the purpose of the skeleton in humans and animals.

Chemistry

Rocks

- Compare and group rocks based on their appearance and physical properties, giving a reason.
- Describe how fossils are formed.
- Describe how soil is made.
- Describe and explain the difference between sedimentary and igneous rock.

Physics

Light

- Describe what dark is (the absence of light).
- Explain that light is needed in order to see.
- Explain that light is reflected from a surface.
- Explain and demonstrate how a shadow is formed.
- Explore shadow size and explain.
- Explain the danger of direct sunlight and describe how to keep protected.

Forces and magnets

- Explore and describe how objects move on different surfaces.
- Explain how some forces require contact and some do not, giving examples.
- Explore and explain how objects attract and repel in relation to objects and other magnets.
- Predict whether objects will be magnetic and carry out an enquiry to test this out.
- Describe how magnets work.
- Predict whether magnets will attract or repel and give a reason.

Science

By the end of Year 4 - learners should be able to:

A year 4 scientist

Working scientifically (Y3 and Y4)

- Ask relevant scientific questions.
- Use observations and knowledge to answer scientific questions.
- Set up a simple enquiry to explore a scientific question.
- Set up a test to compare two things.
- Set up a fair test and explain why it is fair.
- Make careful and accurate observations, including the use of standard units.
- Use equipment, including thermometers and data loggers to make measurements.
- Gather, record, classify and present data in different ways to answer scientific questions.
- Use diagrams, keys, bar charts and tables; using scientific language.
- Use findings to report in different ways, including oral and written explanations, presentation.
- Draw conclusions and suggest improvements.
- Make a prediction with a reason.
- Identify differences, similarities and changes related to an enquiry.

Biology

Living things and their habitats

- Group living things in different ways.
- Use classification keys to group, identify and name living things.
- Create classification keys to group, identify and name living things (for others to use).
- Describe how changes to an environment could endanger living things.

Animals, including humans

- Identify and name the parts of the human digestive system.
- Describe the functions of the organs in the human digestive system.
- Identify and describe the different types of teeth in humans.
- Describe the functions of different human teeth.
- Use food chains to identify producers, predators and prey.
- Construct food chains to identify producers, predators and prey.

Chemistry

States of matter

- Group materials based on their state of matter (solid, liquid, gas).
- Describe how some materials can change state.
- Explore how materials change state.
- Measure the temperature at which materials change state.
- Describe the water cycle.
- Explain the part played by evaporation and condensation in the water cycle.

Physics

Sound

- Describe how sound is made.
- Explain how sound travels from a source to our ears.
- Explain the place of vibration in hearing.
- Explore the correlation between pitch and the object producing a sound.
- Explore the correlation between the volume of a sound and the strength of the vibrations that produced it.
- Describe what happens to a sound as it travels away from its source.

Electricity

- Identify and name appliances that require electricity to function.
- Construct a series circuit.
- Identify and name the components in a series circuit (including cells, wires, bulbs, switches and buzzers).
- Draw a circuit diagram.
- Predict and test whether a lamp will light within a circuit.
- Describe the function of a switch in a circuit.
- Describe the difference between a conductor and insulators; giving examples of each.

Science

By the end of Year 5 - learners should be able to:

A year 5 scientist

Working scientifically (Y5 and Y6)	Biology	Chemistry	Physics
• Plan different types of scientific enquiry.	**Living things and their habitats**	**Properties and changes of materials**	**Earth and space**
• Control variables in an enquiry.	• Describe the life cycle of different living things, e.g. mammal, amphibian, insect bird.	• Compare and group materials based on their properties (e.g. hardness, solubility, transparency, conductivity, [electrical & thermal], and response to magnets).	• Describe and explain the movement of the Earth and other planets relative to the Sun.
• Measure accurate and precisely using a range of equipment.	• Describe the differences between different life cycles.	• Describe how a material dissolves to form a solution; explaining the process of dissolving.	• Describe and explain the movement of the Moon relative to the Earth.
• Record data and results using scientific diagrams and labels, classification keys, tables, scatter graphs, bar and line graphs.	• Describe the process of reproduction in plants.	• Describe and show how to recover a substance from a solution.	• Explain and demonstrate how night and day are created.
• Use the outcome of test results to make predictions and set up a further comparative fair test.	• Describe the process of reproduction in animals.	• Describe how some materials can be separated.	• Describe the Sun, Earth and Moon (using the term spherical).
• Report findings from enquiries in a range of ways.	**Animals, including humans**	• Demonstrate how materials can be separated (e.g. through filtering, sieving and evaporating).	**Forces**
• Explain a conclusion from an enquiry.	• Create a timeline to indicate stages of growth in humans.	• Know and can demonstrate that some changes are reversible and some are not.	• Explain what gravity is and its impact on our lives.
• Explain causal relationships in an enquiry.		• Explain how some changes result in the formation of a new material and that this is usually irreversible.	• Identify and explain the effect of air resistance.
• Relate the outcome from an enquiry to scientific knowledge in order to state whether evidence supports or refutes an argument or theory.		• Discuss reversible and irreversible changes.	• Identify and explain the effect of water resistance.
• Read, spell and pronounce scientific vocabulary accurately.		• Give evidenced reasons why materials should be used for specific purposes.	• Identify and explain the effect of friction.
			• Explain how levers, pulleys and gears allow a smaller force to have a greater effect.